FOR SIGNS AND SEASONS

A Primer on the
Church Calendar

DUANE GARNER

FOR SIGNS
AND SEASONS

For Signs and Seasons
A Primer on the Church Calendar

Copyright © 2024 by Duane Garner

Athanasius Press
715 Cypress Street
West Monroe, Louisiana, 71291
athanasiuspress.org | (318) 323-3061

ISBN: 978-1-957726-19-9

Cover design and typesetting: Rachel Rosales
Special thanks to Samantha Parker

All scripture citations are taken from the NKJV unless otherwise noted.

Prayer texts taken from *The Book of Common Worship*, 1946 edition, and *The Shorter Prayer Book*, 1946, an abbreviation of *The Book of Common Prayer.*

Printed in the United States of America.

Contents

Introduction

And God said, "Let there be lights in the expanse of the heavens to separate the day from the night, and let them be for signs and for seasons, and days and years."
—Genesis 1:14

As I write this, it is the autumn of the year 2024. 2024 years since what? When did we start counting years when we did? It is *Anno Domini 2024,* "the year of our Lord 2024," or 2,024 years since the birth of Jesus. Everyone in the modern world— from the atheist to the Buddhist to the Muslim to the agnostic to the polytheist—is forced to recognize the life of Jesus of Nazareth every time they write a check, sign a contract, or make an appointment. They acknowledge, whether they like it or not, that the events of His life are the most important events in history, that they irreversibly changed the world, and that because of this, Jesus is the Lord of history. He is Lord of time itself. All of creation—even the seasons and the passing of years— points to the lordship of Jesus over all things.

Because we are His people, we care about history, and therefore we care about time. We mark time so that we can redeem time. The courses of the sun, moon, and stars and the changing of the seasons are not irrelevant to us. They are not simply mundane aspects of this creaturely existence which we hope to shed someday when we become disembodied spirits. The faithful care about these things, because through these things God has revealed Himself.

"Teach Us to Number Our Days"

In Psalm 90, Moses meditates on the passage of time and the brevity of our lives, contrasted with the eternal steadfastness of Yahweh. He prays that we might be faithful to carefully steward the few days we have, numbering them in a way that is pleasing to God in order that we might learn wisdom.

Moses lived a great long time and spent most of those days waiting. His life was marked by brief periods of intense action interspersed with long periods of faithful, patient obedience. We can relate to that. Occasionally, we have some pretty exciting days, and some pretty disastrous days, but most of our lives are even-keeled: a little bad, a little good. Moses had three forty-year-long stretches of preparation, each capped by a great event.

Moses waited patiently the first forty years of his life, growing and learning in Pharaoh's house, looking for his purpose and his opportunity to serve his own people who were in bondage. He jumped at the opportunity to deliver one of them who was being physically beaten. In the process of defending him, he killed the assailant, but the people of Israel mocked him for it. They were not yet ready for their deliverance. So Moses went and spent the next forty years in the wilderness with sheep, in preparation for when he would later spend forty years in the wilderness with sheep of the two-legged variety. He married a girl and took care of her father's animals. One day, he saw a burning bush and there God commissioned him to return to Egypt and bring Israel out of bondage. God delivered His people, carried them through the Red Sea to Mt. Sinai, and gave them His law, with orders to go take the land of Canaan. Yet the people refused to obey, and so Moses and the people spent the next forty years wandering in the wilderness, waiting for the next generation to grow up so that they could go in and take the land.

It appears Moses wrote Psalm 90 near the end of his life, reflecting on the past 120 years or so, seeing how fast they had gone, how quickly those years had run through his fingers. He compared our short lives to the eternity of God. Moses wrote that we get seventy years, eighty if we are really blessed. If we think that time goes quickly, how much shorter our lives must seem from God's vantage point. When Moses sings "A thousand years in your sight are like a day that has just gone by, or like a watch in the night," he is not proposing that time does not matter to God, but that God has a perspective on time that we cannot begin to fathom.

Later, Peter picked up this theme to comfort the churches by encouraging them to be patient and endure suffering because "with the Lord one day is as a thousand years, and a thousand years as one day" (2 Peter 3:8). This is not a mathematical formula. This is a declaration that God does not share our perspective about time. When we think a particular blessing or deliverance is taking forever, God has prepared the answer right around the corner. When we see our lives flying before our eyes, and our children growing so fast, He sees all the details and all the fractals and branches of every detail that He is working out.

God has committed a number of days to each of us. He expects us to be faithful stewards of those days. In light of the fleeting nature of our lives, the fact that we are like grass that shoots up and gets cut down, Moses prays, "teach us to number our days, that we may gain a heart of wisdom" (Psalm 90:12). The faithful ought to care about time, to mark time, so that we can redeem time.

Because time is precious, we must plan our time and not waste it. Moses prays, "satisfy us early with Your mercy, that we may rejoice and be glad all our days" (v. 14), and "establish the work of our hands for us; yes, establish the work of our hands" (v. 17). Here we see that time is redeemed in two ways: first, in rejoicing—in worship, in celebration, in festivity, and feasting—and second, in work—work to provide food for our houses, work to educate and train our children, work to provide for others. We keep both in view before us. There is so much work that there never seems to be enough time. Yet we understand that work isn't everything. We also redeem our time through worship and feasting, since they, too, are indispensable ways to number our days with wisdom.

Of Time and In Time

From very early in Church history, Christians understood that one important way we number our days is by stopping at special occasions and rejoicing in the events of the life of Jesus. When the Church sets aside time for the important business of rejoicing and celebration, we celebrate *real* events that happened in time, in history. We don't celebrate a philosophy, timeless morals, or a political system. Our faith is founded upon *factual historical events*, not on theories, ideas, or constructs.

History matters to the Christian faith because it is rooted in time, with real people, places, and events *in time*. The gospel is rooted *in time* because it is the account of *historical* events. The gospel writers give us chronological markers such as "in the time of Herod," "in the time of Caesar Augustus," "on this day, these things happened." God's work in history means that history is relevant and meaningful to us. Since our faith is rooted in time, it is by the faithful preaching of the gospel that time is redeemed and claimed. Jesus does not rescue us from time and history, but from sin and death, so that we can reclaim all those things for His glory. We aren't saved *from* time, but *in* time. We can now consecrate our time and reclaim it for God. To pagans and unbelievers history appears to repeat itself. For them, no time is more relevant than the present, and there is no greater story being played out in time. History has no goal or aim. It is just one thing after another. However, the faithful know that time has a goal and a purpose, and that all of history is flowing into a glorious future. Time is not a curse, nor a result of the curse. Time was built into the order of the world in the creation week, and the entire cosmos is designed in such a way to aid us in marking out God's works in history. God's people have always used calendars, chronologies, and histories to commemorate God's mighty acts on our behalf.

A Festal World

At creation, God said, "Let there be lights in the firmament of the heavens to divide the day from the night; and let them be for signs and seasons, and for days and years" (Genesis 1:14). It is important to note that God designed all of this before the Fall. Seasons and the marking of time are not ways that we manage the effects of the curse. Before Adam's sin, God intended for there to be a cycle of spring, summer, autumn, and winter. He intended for the heavenly bodies to mark our time and mankind has always used the lights above as a celestial calendar. It is inescapable. A year is one trip around the sun. A month is one cycle of the moon. Not only are the heavenly bodies for the marking of days and years, but God also said "let them be for signs and seasons." The word translated "seasons" here is not only referring to summertime and wintertime. This word is used two hundred times throughout the Old Testament for festival seasons and special times for worship. God set up the stars, sun, and moon in their courses to let us know when it is time to celebrate, rejoice, and give thanks. The creation guides us in how to reflect upon His work of grace and redemption. The cycles of the year tell the story of the gospel.

After the Lord redeemed Israel from Egypt, He prescribed Israel's festival seasons and the feasts in a calendar synchronized with the seasons of the year (Leviticus 23). The word "feasts" in Leviticus is the same word "seasons" from Genesis 1. In the spring, they were to celebrate Passover with its theme of deliverance. Just as the trees and plants and earth moved from death to life, so they would be reminded that God has brought them from death to life. In the summer, they would celebrate Pentecost. Summer is the season of growth, maturation, fruition.

During this time they were to celebrate the giving of the Law by which they would grow through the Spirit. Then, in the fall, they held the Feast of Tabernacles. While they were gathering in the harvest and thanking God for His provision, they would be pointed to that final spiritual harvest of all the nations.

In addition to these three seasons, they had the weekly Sabbath and other feasts such as harvest festivals, and other celebrations they picked up along the way. As Israel moved through history, they found that God gave them more reasons to celebrate and they were apparently free to add to the calendar of festivals. In Esther we read about a great deliverance of God's people that resulted in the holiday of Purim, where gifts were exchanged. This indicates that gift-giving is not some licentious practice borrowed from the pagans. Later, in the period between the Old and New Testaments, there was another deliverance during the time of the Maccabees, and out of that came the celebration of Hanukkah. In John 10:22 we find Jesus at the temple during the winter at "the Feast of Dedication" which eventually became known as "Hanukkah." As a Jewish boy from a faithful family, Jesus would have kept all of His people's feasts, including Purim and Hanukkah. If it was permissible for Jesus to enjoy the entire calendar of Jewish festivals—both those instituted directly by God and those His people instituted to praise Him for his deliverance—then why should we not celebrate His birth, His life, and His resurrection?

Jesus Changes Our Time

Because Jesus has now fulfilled all the things to which those Old Testament feasts pointed, and because the Church has been designated as the new humanity with and under Jesus, we have taken dominion over time with new festivals and feasts that celebrate the fulfillment of the old covenant. From very early in her history, the Church established a new calendar which arranges our festival times around the events in the life of Jesus.

We begin our calendar with the great cycle of **Advent, Christmas,** and **Epiphany.** This season focuses both on the first and future comings of Jesus, and all the ways He revealed himself to be the light of the world. The second great season is that of **Easter**, which includes **Lent, Holy Week, Easter,** and **Ascension.** The third great season is the long one of **Pentecost**, in which we focus on the maturation and growth of the Church by the work of the Spirit. It includes the feast days of **Pentecost**, **Trinity Sunday**, and **All Saints' Day**.

All of creation helps to tell the story. In the grand drama of the heavens above and the changing of the seasons below, the narrative unfolds. Advent and Christmas come at the close of the year, where, in the northern hemisphere, everything is dying, everything is winding down, there is less and less light. If this were the first time you had experienced winter, you would think that the world was ending. It looks like darkness has the victory. Everything is dead and cold and gray.

But then, when the days are at their darkest, everything begins to turn the other way toward warmth and life, and the light gets stronger. It is during this time when we celebrate the birth of Jesus. Jesus came at the darkest time, where it looked like everything was really over for Israel—no revelation, no hope, no future. Death reigned over the whole world, but then here came Jesus, the Daystar, and He fought back against the darkness. During the season of Epiphany, when we rejoice in all the ways Jesus was revealed to be the Light of the world, shining the light of the gospel to all the nations, we look outside and see that the light begins to gradually overtake the darkness. Day by day the sunlight lasts longer, but it is going to take time for the sun to have its full effect.

In the mid- to late-winter, the light has come, but the trees are still dormant; there are no flowers or fruit. During the season of Lent, we remember the sufferings of Jesus. We remember that He was the light of the world, but that the world didn't receive Him. We remember our own sins which were the cause of His suffering. As Lent winds down, suddenly everything around us comes to life. There's life everywhere—flowers and leaves on the trees, and green grass and birds and bees, boys proposing to girls, and weddings and babies. It's the time of resurrection, and, indeed, Jesus' resurrection brings new life to the whole world.

When we move to summer, a time of growth and fruit bearing and a time of maturation, we find ourselves in the season of Pentecost. We celebrate the pouring out of the Holy Spirit and acknowledge the way that He grows up humanity, reforms it, and shapes it. At the end of the season of Pentecost comes the harvest, which points us to the final harvest and judgment. There we wrap back around to Advent, beginning our cycle again.

The seasons play the story out for us, and they do this every year, repeating their rhythms. This arrangement is not necessary. God did not have to make things this way. We do not have to have seasons, or even weather. It could be sunny and 72° with a gentle breeze every day, but God did not desire it to be that way. There are hot days and cold days, clear days and cloudy days, soft breezes and great storms. Beautiful sunny days that make you wish to run and roll in the grass; and dark, gloomy, cloudy rainy days that make you wish to stay inside and not stick your head out. Our lives also have sunny days and dark days. We have days where we experience unbelievable joy and success, and we have days where life is tough and painful. Our lives and all of history go through cycles. Creation goes through cycles, and this is how God wills it to be. It is through these cycles that we and the world grow and mature and move from glory to glory.

Why a Church Calendar?

Redeeming the time through a cyclical festival calendar helps us to realize that festivals, feast days, and holidays are not simply to give children something fun to do. They are not silly reasons to decorate the house, or eat something different—things that we could really take or leave. In our very pragmatic world, we might think of holidays as kind of short break from work. We eat, we give presents, take off work a day or two, but then get back to our real life, the really important stuff. Because, after all, holidays truly are impractical, with all of their fuss and expense. You might be tempted to think, "Maybe this year I ought to just skip the whole thing." This sounds like a serious, no-nonsense approach, but in reality this is warped and upside-down. Festivity is serious business. Whether or not you celebrate the most important events in the history of the world is not a peripheral matter. God commanded His people Israel to follow a certain calendar of feast days and celebrations, by which He indicated they must stop doing what they were doing, and especially to stop all their work, because these were His days. They were to be prepared to set aside their time and their money, because they were to have a party when He told them to have a party. They must buy meat and wine and bread, and to sing and laugh and dance and cut up. This "non-sense" is, in fact, essential for God's people, then and now.

Following the Church calendar does so many things for us, providing experiences and perspectives that we sometimes cannot even articulate. Here are just three of the many benefits.

First, following the calendar of feast days disciplines us in joy and festivity. There may be years where you do not feel like celebrating this or that. You have had a tough year. You lost someone special. You are battling illness and you just do not have it in you. But these are fixed days. You don't get to choose when they are coming. When the day comes you are called to rejoice on that day, just like you are called to worship. God calls you to rise above your sorrows and celebrate, in spite of your situation, acknowledging God's work throughout your whole life and not letting sorrows, which we acknowledge to be temporary, to obscure that. Because Jesus has come, because He has been resurrected, because He has poured out His spirit, and all of human history is headed toward that great harvest, everything is going to be fine. In fact, they are going to be better than fine. We need to be happy about that.

These celebrations teach us to see sorrow and bitter providences as temporary and part of the cycle of life. By them we put into action our knowledge that these bad things in life are just chapters in a bigger story of which we are a part. They provide a narrative to those long days of waiting and wondering when the next big thing is going to come, when we think we are not getting anywhere. The cycle of celebrations reminds us, no, you are going somewhere, and the church is going somewhere, and everything is moving and improving and reforming in ways you cannot see because you don't have God's perspective on time. Trust that, although it is winter now, spring is coming. It comes every year. God said after the flood, "While the earth remains, seedtime and harvest, cold and heat, winter and summer, and day and night shall not cease" (Genesis 8:22). Do not despair. Spring is coming.

Second, this calendar gives us an identity and a culture. The Western world is reverting to a kind of tribalism. Because everyone feels disconnected from the whole, and the culture is so splintered, people grasp for some kind of identity and shared history. People united to Jesus do not have to go looking for a culture or a tradition; we have those things, and we have the only substantial, real, lasting, redeeming story available to mankind. The calendar shapes us into a people with one mind and one heart. Our holidays are reference points indicating who we are and what is most important to us. They remind us of what is at the center of life. For Israel, their feast days identified who they were: they were delivered people. So, too, our feast days remind us that we are members of the body of Christ. We mark time by the events of His life, and every year we remind ourselves of those events together, by singing them back and forth to each other, by reading them and hearing them, and it never gets old. Each time we hear it, it's like the first time. Our calendar gives us an identity.

And third, our calendar tells us the story of the gospel. Through re-enacting the grand drama of the seasons and the feast days, we show the world that we believe the gospel. Jesus' people have been and ought still be known for deep, unshakable, irrepressible joy. No matter what is going on in the world, we stop on feast days and determine that we will be really happy. We say to the world, "Don't you want to be a part of this? Stop borrowing the things from us that you like and crafting your own counterfeit. Come be part of the real deal."

Living in covenant with the Creator of the universe and with His people is the happiest thing in the world. I want everyone around me to understand that. I want my children to understand that. I want them to know the covenant as the happiest place on earth. In the fellowship of the church we have all the best that life has to offer—this is where the fun is. What's out there, whatever it is, can't even come close to what we have here. People outside the covenant think they are having fun, but in their idolatry and rebellion they are robbing themselves of true joy and destroying each other. This is the place of life. This is the place of fulfillment of all your heart's desires. This is deep abiding everlasting light and joy.

Let us be earnestly tenacious and unyielding about our feast days. Let us determine to enjoy them and enjoy all of them. Let us be dead serious about expressing our joy in the God who gave us life through His son Jesus through *all* the days and seasons and years He has given us.

Advent

Lift up your heads, O you gates!
And the King of glory shall come in.
—Psalm 24:7

What Is Advent?

The English word *advent* is derived from the Latin verb *advenire*, "to come to, arrive." The focus of the season of Advent is on all the ways that the Lord draws near to judge the earth, to deliver His people, and to set things right. The Lord *has come* to us at the birth of Christ, *presently comes* to us especially on the Lord's Day, and *will come* to us bodily again in the future judgment and resurrection. All of these comings are in view and are the subjects of our reflection, singing, and praying through the Sundays of Advent.

The purpose of the season of Advent is not to imagine ourselves to be living at the time immediately preceding Christ's birth and somehow pretending

1

that we are waiting for Him to be born. It is not time for a spiritual game of "make believe." Neither is the purpose of Advent to think sentimental thoughts about the baby Jesus. "Advent" is not another name for "the Christmas shopping season."

In the season of Advent we pray for the coming of the Lord as we remember His first coming and how He faithfully kept the promises He made to His people in the Hebrew Scriptures. We pray that He will draw near to us continually, judging the enemies of the Church, vindicating His name and His Church, and delivering His people from all evil. During the Advent season we petition the Lord to come again to us, both now and finally at the end of the age. We switch the sanctuary colors to royal purple, marking our expectation of the coming King.

The Advent Readings

These Bible readings emphasize the Lord's coming in judgment and salvation. You should read Isaiah, for example, remembering that the Lord kept His word and came to His people. He sent the Assyrians and Babylonians to chastise them for their unrepentant ways. He also came to them after the exile, as He promised, to return them to their land.

The Lord promises similar judgment on His people in the New Testament if they reach the same level of spiritual dullness that Israel did (Revelation 3:14–22). The New Testament readings all refer either to the Lord Jesus' historical coming in judgment upon apostate Israel in AD 70 or His final coming at the end of the age. "Judgment begins in the house of God" (1 Peter 4:17). Ultimately, the Lord came to His people in Jesus Christ in order to forgive our sins (Matthew 1:21), and He will come again as our King to accomplish our comprehensive deliverance from evil.

Look for the connection between the Old and New Testament readings. They will usually have a common theme centered on the coming of the Lord in judgment and salvation. The psalms selected for this season are prayers for deliverance in anticipation of the coming of the King.

A BRIEF ORDER FOR
ADVENT FAMILY DEVOTIONS

Opening Psalm
The family may begin by singing one of the following psalms: 2, 22, 23, 24, 29, 47, 66, 72, 76, 80, 98, 99, 100, 122, 124, 148

Opening Prayer
Leader: Let us pray.

First Week in Advent

All: Stir up, we implore You, Your power, O Lord, and come, that by Your protection we may be rescued from the threatening perils of our sins and be saved by Your mighty deliverance: for You live and reign with the Father and the Holy Ghost, one God, now and forever. Amen!

Second Week in Advent

All: Stir up our hearts, O Lord, to make ready the way of your only-begotten Son that at His second coming we may worship Him in purity, who lives and reigns with You and the Holy Ghost, one God, now and forever. Amen!

Third Week in Advent

All: Stir up Your power, O Lord, and come alongside us with great might; and because we are sorely hindered by our sins, let Your bountiful grace and mercy speedily help and deliver us: through Jesus Christ, our Lord, who lives and reigns with You and the Holy Ghost, one God, now and forever. Amen!

Fourth Week in Advent & Christmas

All: O God, who makes us glad with the yearly remembrance of the birth of Your only Son Jesus Christ; grant that as we joyfully receive Him for our redeemer, so we may with sure confidence behold Him when He comes to be our judge, who lives and reigns with You and the Holy Ghost, one God, world without end. Amen!

Lighting the Advent Candle

If the family uses an Advent wreath, the appropriate candles may be lit at this time.

Scripture Readings

First Week in Advent

Isaiah 1:1–20; 1 Thess. 1:1–10; Psalm 122
Isaiah 1:21–31; 1 Thess. 2:1–12; Psalm 72
Isaiah 2:1–11; 1 Thess. 2:13–20; Psalm 23
Isaiah 2:5–22; 1 Thess. 3:1–13; Psalm 118
Isaiah 3:1–4:1; 1 Thess. 4:1–12; Psalm 98
Isaiah 4:2–6; 1 Thess. 4:13–18; Psalm 147
(Optional Sunday: Isaiah 43:1–13; Psalm 46)

Second Week in Advent

Isaiah 7:1–17; 1 Thess. 5:1–11; Psalm 85
Isaiah 8:11–9:1; 1 Thess. 5:12–28; Psalm 19

Isaiah 9:2–12; 2 Thess. 1:1–12; Psalm 103
Isaiah 11:1–16; 2 Thess. 2:1–12; Psalm 145
Isaiah 12:1–6; 2 Thess. 2:13–3:5; Psalm 1
Isaiah 24:1–23; 2 Thess. 3:6–18; Psalm 80
(Optional Sunday: Isaiah 46; Romans 15:4–13; Psalm 9)

Third Week in Advent

Isaiah 25:1–12; 2 Peter 1:1–11; Psalm 72
Isaiah 28:9–22; 2 Peter 1:12–21; Psalm 71
Isaiah 29:13–24; 2 Peter 2:1–10; Psalm 24
Isaiah 33:10–24; 2 Peter 2:11–16; Psalm 33
Isaiah 62:1–12; 2 Peter 2:17–22; Psalm 34
Isaiah 64:1–12; 2 Peter 3:1–18; Psalm 25
(Optional Sunday: Isaiah 25; 1 Cor. 3:16–4:5; Psalm 75)

Fourth Week in Advent

Zechariah 2:10–13; Luke 1:39–56; Psalm 98
Revelation 21:9–21; Luke 1:57–79; Psalm 31
Revelation 21:22–22:5; Luke 2:1–14; Psalm 97
Revelation 22:6–21; Luke 2:25–35; Psalm 100
Revelation 1:1–8; John 1:1–18; Psalm 96
Isaiah 40:1–31; 1 John 4:7–16; Psalm 106
(Optional Sunday: Isaiah 35; Philemon 4:4–9; Psalm 97)

Hymn

*In the **first through third weeks** of Advent, select one of the following Advent hymns.*

(Below are the well-known titles or first lines of the suggested hymns. They may be found in many hymnals or online at hymn sites such as *hymnary.org*, which is an excellent resource for lyrics, image files, and audio recordings of these hymns.)

- Arise, Sons of the Kingdom
- Behold, the Bridegroom Cometh
- Come, Thou Long Expected Jesus
- Come, Thou Precious Ransom, Come
- Comfort, Comfort Ye My People
- Hark! a Thrilling Voice Is Sounding
- Hark, the Glad Sound, the Savior Comes
- Hills of the North, Rejoice
- How Lovely Shines the Morning Star!
- Jesus Came, the Heavens Adoring
- Lift Up Your Heads
- Lo! He Comes with Clouds Descending
- Magnificat
- O Bride of Christ, Rejoice!
- O Come, O Come, Emmanuel
- O Savior, Rend the Heavens Wide
- Prepare the Way, O Zion
- Rejoice, All Ye Believers

- Savior of the Nations, Come
- The Advent of Our King
- The Bridegroom Soon Will Call Us
- The King Shall Come When Morning Dawns
- The Race that Long in Darkness Pined
- Thy Kingdom Come on Bended Knee
- Wake, Awake, for Night Is Flying

*In the **fourth week** of Advent, the following Christmas hymns are appropriate:*

- Angels We Have Heard on High
- From Heaven Above to Earth I Come
- God Rest Ye Merry, Gentlemen
- Good Christian Men, Rejoice
- Hark! the Herald Angels Sing
- Joy to the World! the Lord Is Come
- Let All Mortal Flesh Keep Silence
- Lo, How a Rose E'er Blooming
- O Come, All Ye Faithful
- O Little Town of Bethlehem
- Of the Father's Love Begotten
- Silent Night, Holy Night
- Sing, O Sing, This Blessed Morn
- The First Noel
- What Child Is This

Prayer Requests & Closing Prayer

Family members may make specific prayer requests, after which the entire family can pray.

Leader: The almighty and merciful God, the Father, the Son, and the Holy Spirit, bless us and keep us.

All: Amen!

Christmas

Glory to God in the highest,
And on earth peace, goodwill toward men!
—Luke 2:14

All the Twelve Days of Christmas

As we bring the Advent season to a close, we exchange the "preparatory purple" of Advent for "celebratory white" as we begin the full twelve-day feast of Christmastide.

This season begins on Christmas Eve and goes all the way to Epiphany on January 6. There are traditions and a special significance assigned to many of the days within that twelve day stretch. In fact, centuries ago, people would wait until Epiphany to exchange gifts, and do many little things along the way during the Christmas season to build up to the great feast of Epiphany.

As Christians try to recover many of the traditions we have lost, there has been a renewed interest in understanding and celebrating throughout the whole Christmas season. One idea for celebrating the twelve days is to leave your decorations and lights up until Epiphany. They are Christmas decorations, after all, and Christmas isn't over on December 26. The party is just getting started. This is sure to prompt interesting conversations with your neighbors when they see your lights still up in January.

Another general principle, especially if you have children at home, is to do some small, special thing every day to mark the days of the season. It does not always work out perfectly, but try to find one special thing to do every day of the season as a way to keep up the cheer—whether it is going somewhere as a family you do not normally go, or having special foods and drinks you don't normally enjoy, or saving a small present or two to give on a later day of the season.

To assist your planning, here is a schedule that can be adapted to serve different traditions and families.

First Day of Christmas
Christmas Day

Begin the Christmas season with gifts and feasting and your usual family traditions.

Collect for the day:

O God, who makes us glad with the yearly remembrance of the birth of Your only Son Jesus Christ; grant that as we joyfully receive Him for our redeemer, so we may with sure confidence behold Him when He comes to be our judge, who lives and reigns with You and the Holy Ghost, one God, world without end. Amen!

Second Day of Christmas
St. Stephen's Day/Boxing Day

This is the Feast of Stephen, the first martyr for Christ and a deacon who was set apart to care for the poor. In memory of his faith and example, we look for opportunities today to bless those who are not as well-off as we are. Christians throughout history have used the second day of Christmas to give leftovers from their feasts to the poor. As the children bring new Christmas toys into their rooms, and as you add new clothes to your closet, maybe it is a good time to bag up some old gently-used things and donate them. Charity can take many forms, but however you have opportunity, be sure to sing the St. Stephen's Day Carol "Good King Wenceslaus" as you do it.

Collect for the day:

Grant, O Lord, that, in all our suffering here on earth for the testimony of Your truth, we may steadfastly look up to heaven, and by faith behold the glory that shall be revealed; and, being filled by the Holy Ghost, may learn to love and bless our persecutors by the example of Your first martyr, Stephen, who prayed for his murderers to You, O blessed Jesus, who stands at the right hand of God to comfort and aid all those who suffer for You, our only mediator and advocate. Amen!

Third Day of Christmas
Feast of St. John the Evangelist

Gather with friends to celebrate the feast of St. John. Remember, John was the apostle who wrote "We know that we have passed from death to life, because we love the brethren," and "Beloved, let us love one another, for love is of God; and everyone who loves is born of God and knows God." One old custom on this feast day is to manifest that fellowship and love around a good bottle of wine, to bless it and give thanks to God for the "wine which gladdens the heart of man" and for the joy we have in our communion together.

Collect for the day:

Merciful Lord, we ask You to cast Your bright beams of light upon Your church, that it, being illuminated by the writings of Your blessed apostle and evangelist John, may so walk in the light of Your truth, that it may at length attain to life everlasting; through Jesus Christ our Lord. Amen!

Fourth Day of Christmas
Feast of the Innocents

This is a day to remember Herod's slaughter of the Hebrew children in imitation of Pharaoh's similar wickedness. The Serpent has always tried to kill the Seed of the Woman, and thus has always made war on children. His warfare continues today. Our response to this is to give thanks for our children, to delight in the gift of childhood, and to sing the imprecatory psalms against the Serpent and his minions who would destroy children. One enjoyable custom on this day is to allow the youngest child in the household to choose the day's food, drink, music, and entertainment.

Fifth & Sixth Days of Christmas

These are quiet days on the church calendar, but good days to get caught up on whatever you were not able to get done earlier in the season. These are great days to work on Christmas cards, thank-you cards, and other Christmas-time correspondence.

Seventh Day of Christmas
New Year's Eve

The seventh day of Christmas is always the last day of the year, and it is customary on this day to reflect on all the ways that God has blessed us, protected us, corrected us, provided for us, and sanctified us in the last year.

Give thanks and rejoice for another year of life under the sun, and for the manifold blessings of being God's image-bearers living in this amazing world He has created for us. The traditional drink for this time of year is a punch called "wassail" (from the Saxon *was haile* meaning "to your health"). Wassail is a hot spiced cider. There are many recipes available in cookbooks and on the internet. Even without the special punch, when friends come "wassailing" on New Year's Eve and New Year's Day, drink in joy and say a prayer for good health in the coming year.

Eighth Day of Christmas
New Year's Day/Feast of the Circumcision of Jesus

Remember that Mary and Joseph were faithful to God's Law and brought the infant Jesus to be circumcised on the eighth day after his birth (Luke

2:21). Jesus was fully obedient to God's Law every step of the way, all through His life, and there was nothing in His life that someone could point to as evidence that He was not a faithful Jew. Because we are united to Him by faith, His faithfulness is our faithfulness, His obedience is our obedience; and every thing that He does, He does for His people. So as He was circumcised and submitted to His Father's law every day of His life, He fulfilled and obeyed perfectly the law which we fail to uphold and submit to in our sin and rebellion. On the basis of His obedience, and because we are His, so now His acceptance before God the Father is our acceptance before God the Father.

The eighth day of His life was also when He was given the name "Jesus" or "Yeshua"—"Yahweh saves"—because, as the angel said to Mary, "He will save His people." For all of these things we rejoice and give thanks this eighth day of Christmas! Even before He could talk or walk, Jesus was beginning His saving work on our behalf, delivering us from our sins.

One fun dinner conversation to have tonight is to rehearse the origin of everyone's name—not only its meaning, but also whom each was named after, or the story of how you decided upon each child's name. Then tell the story of each person's baptism, and talk about when they were brought into covenant with God, just as Jesus' parents were faithful to bring him into the covenant when He was a child. Also, this is a good day to sing the Song of Simeon, the man who burst out in praise the day that Mary and Joseph brought Jesus to the temple on that eighth day.

Collect for the day:
Almighty God, who made Your blessed Son to be circumcised, and obedient to the law for men; grant us the true circumcision of the Spirit; that our hearts—and all our bodies—being made dead to all worldly lusts, we may in all things obey Your will; through Your Son Jesus Christ. Amen!

Ninth Day of Christmas

This is a good night to get together with other families, bring instruments, and sing and play Christmas songs and other favorites. As the Christmas season winds down, recall the great Christmases of your family's past. What was the most memorable present you ever received? What was the funniest thing that ever happened at Christmas? What were some traditions that you grew up with that you might try next year?

Tenth & Eleventh Days of Christmas

This is another quiet set of days on the calendar; they are good days to give each other any small trinkets or candy or special little treats you have held back. Perhaps the children could work on little plays, presentations, poems, or songs to perform for the family.

Twelfth Day of Christmas
Twelfth Night/The Final Day of Celebration

Traditionally, this has been the day of the biggest party of the season, where everyone breaks out the cakes, pies, and all the best wine. As you take down the greenery and the Christmas trees you have the makings of a great bonfire. If you have been saving any presents, now is the time to give them, and close out the Christmas season with a bang.

Epiphany

Arise, shine; for your light has come!
And the glory of the Lord is risen upon you.
—Isaiah 60:1

Epiphany is a time when we celebrate all the ways that Jesus was revealed to be the Savior of the Nations. "Epiphany" comes from the Greek word for "revelation" or "manifestation," and this is the time of the year where we remember those events where Jesus' identity as the Messiah was made manifest.

Jesus was first revealed to nations when the wise men appeared before Him, and this is why Epiphany is also called "Three Kings Day" in some parts of the world. Then, following through His baptism, His miracles, and His transfiguration, the scripture readings, hymns, and prayers of this season walk us through the various manifestations of Jesus' mission throughout His life.

The gospel reading for the Sunday after Epiphany each year takes us to the baptism of Jesus, and so we join with Christians all over the earth in meditating and reflecting on what Jesus' baptism means for us and the world. After the first Sunday of the Epiphany season we switch the sanctuary colors from the bright glorious white to the growing green, reminding us that we are in a "growing season" specifically focusing on the growth of Jesus "in wisdom and stature, in favor with God and men" (Luke 2:52), and on the ever-growing revelation of Jesus to the nations.

A BRIEF ORDER FOR
EPIPHANY FAMILY DEVOTIONS

Opening Psalm
The family may begin by singing one of the following psalms: 2, 8, 46, 72, 96, 97, 100

Opening Prayer
Leader: Let us pray.

All: Everlasting Father, the radiance of faithful souls, who brought the nations to Your light and kings to the brightness of Your rising; fill the world with Your glory, and show Yourself to all the nations, through Him who is the true light and the bright

morning star, Jesus Christ Your son our Lord. Amen!

Scripture Readings
Matt. 2:1–12; Psalm 145; Isa. 49:5–23; Eph. 3

Hymn
Select one of the following Epiphany hymns:

- Arise and Shine in Splendor
- As with Gladness Men of Old
- Brightest and Best
- Let All the Stars in the Skies Give Praise
- What Star Is This with Beams So Bright

Prayer Requests & Closing Prayer
Family members may make specific prayer requests, after which the entire family can pray.

Leader: The grace of the Lord Jesus Christ, and the love of God, and the communion of the Holy Ghost be with us all.

All: Amen!

Lent

So rend your heart, and not your garments;
Return to the Lord your God.
—Joel 2:13

During the season of Lent, we remember the forty days of fasting and temptation Jesus underwent in the wilderness as He battled Satan and suffered on our behalf. The last week of Lent is often referred to as "Holy Week," wherein we walk through the events of the last days of Jesus' earthly ministry leading up to His crucifixion.

This forty-day period (not counting Sundays) before the high feast of Easter has been known for centuries as the season of Lent. "Lent" comes from the old English word *lencten*, which means "spring," and is closely related to the word "length-en," referring to the lengthening days that comes this time of year.

In the ancient Church and in certain parts of the world throughout history, the baptisms of new converts were done on Easter, and thus this season before Easter was traditionally used as a time of catechesis. Converts were instructed in the doctrines of the Christian faith and thus prepared to enter the church not as novices, but as well-trained disciples.

Giving Up Things for Lent?

Because the forty days also bring to mind Jesus' forty-day fast in the wilderness, His battle with Satan, and His suffering on our behalf, Lent has also been used as a time of fasting. When we wage war on our sins and have an acute sense of our own lack of discipline over our minds, tongues, and bodies, it can be appropriate to "go without" certain good things to help us to recall our sinful conditions and the fact that we do not deserve all the good things that God has given us. It is also appropriate to fast in order to pray for our suffering and persecuted brothers and sisters here and around the world.

However, in our day, the fasting aspect of Lent has become something of a joke, with people "giving up" M&Ms or Coke or Facebook during this season. Not only do they give these things up, but they let everyone know that they are giving them up, in direct defiance of Jesus' instruction in

Matthew 6 which requires discretion and privacy when fasting.

The purpose of this season is not to try to become a public martyr for giving up donuts for forty days. The purpose of this season is to reflect on the work of Jesus on our behalf, and to soberly reflect on our own sinful conditions. If fasting assists you, then by all means fast; but fast from food, not merely social media or Netflix, and above all, fast from sinning.

If you choose to fast from food, always break the fast on Sunday. The Lord's Days are not fast days, they are feast days, and Sundays are not included in the season of Lent. You will notice that in various places we refer to Sundays "in" Lent and not Sundays "of" Lent. Sundays are not counted in the forty days of Lent.

It is also helpful to use this as a time of catechesis and training for you and your family. Go through a catechism or confession after supper at night these next forty days. Pick up that fat theology book that you bought several years ago and never had a chance to crack open—divide up the pages by forty and finish it by Easter. Tackle a section of the Bible you are not that familiar with—the prophets or the later histories. Pick a couple of psalms and concentrate on committing them to memory. Or commit yourself to becoming more familiar with the book of Proverbs as a whole.

There are many ways to be discipled by God's Word these forty days, and to enter the Feast of Easter an even stronger and more faithful Christian. You will find the Lenten season to be a sober, but joyful, time of growth and maturation.

The sanctuary colors shift back to the royal purple as we wait for and welcome the victory of our King.

AN ORDER FOR PRIVATE OR FAMILY WORSHIP DURING THE SEASON OF LENT

Leader: In the name of the Father and the Son and the Holy Spirit.

All: Amen!

Sing or read responsively one of the following psalms: 6, 32, 38, 51, 102, 130, 143

Leader: Let us humbly kneel and pray, confessing our sins to Almighty God.

First Week of Lent
All: Most merciful God, we confess that we have sinned against you in thought, word, and deed, by what we have done, and by what we have left undone. We have not loved you with our whole heart; we have not loved our

neighbors as ourselves. We are truly sorry and we humbly repent. For the sake of your Son Jesus Christ, have mercy on us and forgive us; that we may delight in your will, and walk in your ways, to the glory of your Name. Amen.

Second Week of Lent

All: Almighty and most merciful Father, we have erred and strayed from Your ways like lost sheep. We have followed too much the devices and desires of our own hearts. We have offended against Your holy laws. We have left undone those things which we ought to have done; and we have done those things which we ought not to have done; and there is nothing good in us. O Lord, have mercy upon us, miserable offenders. Spare those, O God, who confess their faults. Restore those who are penitent; according to Your promises declared unto men in Christ Jesus our Lord. Grant that we may hereafter live a godly, righteous, and sober life; to the glory of His name. Amen.

Third Week of Lent

All: Eternal God, in whom we live and move and have our being, whose face is hidden from us by our sins, and whose mercy we forget in the blindness of our hearts: cleanse us from all our offenses, and deliver us from proud thoughts and vain desires, that with reverent and humble hearts we may draw near to you, confessing our faults, confiding in your grace, and finding in you our refuge and strength; through Jesus Christ your Son. Amen.

Fourth Week of Lent

All: Gracious God, our sins are too heavy to carry, too real to hide, and too deep to undo. Forgive what our lips tremble to name, what our hearts can no longer bear, and what has become for us a consuming fire of judgment. Set us free from a past that we cannot change; open to us hope in the future where we will be changed; and grant us grace to grow more and more in your likeness and image, through Jesus Christ, the light of the world. Amen.

Fifth Week of Lent

All: Almighty God, since you delay with so much forbearance the punishments which we have deserved and daily draw on ourselves, grant that we may not indulge ourselves but carefully consider how often and in how many different ways we have provoked your wrath against us. May we learn humbly to present ourselves to you for pardon, and with true repentance implore thy mercy. With all our heart we desire to submit ourselves to you, whether you chastise us, or according to your infinite goodness, forgive us. Let our condition be ever blessed, not by flattering ourselves in our apathy, but by finding you to be our kind and bountiful Father, reconciled to us in thine only-begotten Son. Amen.

Sixth Week of Lent

All: Almighty God have mercy on us, forgive us all our sins through our Lord Jesus Christ, strengthen us in all goodness, and by the power of the Holy Spirit keep us in eternal life. Amen.

Leader: Now rise, lift up your heads and hear the good news of God's forgiveness! The Lord is compassionate and gracious, slow to anger and abounding in lovingkindness. He has not dealt with us according to our sins, nor rewarded us according to our iniquities. For as high as the heavens are above the earth, so great is His lovingkindness toward those who fear Him. As far as the east is from the west, so far has He removed our transgressions from us. (*From Psalm 103*)

Read aloud a selection from Scripture, a catechism, a confession, or another helpful book.

Leave time for questions or discussion. Close with a favorite hymn, psalm, or doxology.

Leader: The grace of the Lord Jesus Christ, and the love of God, and the communion of the Holy Spirit be with you all. Amen.

Holy Week

Look! Your king is coming to you:
He is just and having salvation!
—Zechariah 9:9

Palm Sunday

On Palm Sunday we begin the last week of the Lenten season, which we call "Holy Week." Throughout the days leading up to Easter Sunday we mark the final events of the life of the Lord Jesus before His resurrection. The worship services held during latter part of Holy Week—on Maundy Thursday and Good Friday—are understandably more subdued and sober in tone, but the week begins on Sunday with a loud and boisterous "Hosanna!"

The occasion we remember on this day is the grand entrance of Jesus into the city of Jerusalem riding a kingly donkey, where He was met by crowds shouting in praise, waving palm branches and laying their coats on the ground before Him.

The gospels provide this striking scene of the people's acceptance and rejoicing at the start of the week that is quite jarring in contrast to the rejection and persecution which comes at the end of the week. As we commemorate these events, we must keep this emphasis in mind, for while on that day there were certainly many sincere shouts of "Hosanna!" (which means "save," "help," or "deliver"), there were also those in the crowd whose celebration was not altogether a celebration of what Jesus' actual mission was. We have to look under the surface of this palm branch waving—because while the multitudes are shouting "Hosanna" or "Save us" on this day, they are going to be shouting "Crucify him!" a few days later.

Given what we know of the political and social climate of the day, and of the conflicts that Jesus had both with outsiders and His own apostles, it is evident that a good portion of this population was expecting that God had sent them a powerful new military leader who intended to declare war on Rome and the Herods, to liberate Judea, and to bring in a new golden age of Jewish self-rule under a new Jewish kingdom.

They came bearing palm branches because these were a symbol of peace which the Maccabees used centuries before, after their victory over their occupiers. However, they had taken on this nationalistic weight of meaning, as if they were little

Judean flags. The crowd sang Psalm 118 expecting that this Jesus who was riding into Jerusalem on a donkey, like David did, was going to set up His kingly administration in Jerusalem, and they were finally going to be out from under Roman rule. However, this was a misinterpretation of the prophets and a misunderstanding of the role of Messiah.

We know that Jesus was not taking these things at face value because, as Luke reported, Jesus was actually weeping as He entered the city. Jesus said, "If you actually knew the things that make for your peace! But now these things are hidden from your eyes!" All of this enthusiasm will turn on a dime when Jesus goes into the city and does not march up to Herod's doorstep and claim His rule over the city, nor does He declare war on Rome. Instead, He goes into the temple and declares war on the activity there. He drives out the money changers and interrupts their routine of extortion and thievery.

This is also the same day where Jesus rebuked the fig tree and it shriveled up. Like Israel, the fig tree is all leaves, but no fruit. Jesus had palm leaves waved in His face, but there was no real repentance or desire to follow the way that Jesus had laid out for them that would lead them into true peace and life.

As the Church remembers this day through her hymns and prayers and preaching each year, we keep all of these themes in tension. We truly and sincerely sing "Hosanna to the Son of David!" and praise Him as He proceeds into the New Jerusalem, His holy sanctuary. We praise Him as a conquering King for the victory that He has sealed for us. At the same time, we are aware of how often throughout history the mission of Jesus and the Church has been distorted, misinterpreted and co-opted. So we do not ask for salvation or deliverance on our terms, for Jesus to come join us on our plan of self-preservation. We lay down our misguided and uninformed agendas and say, *Lord Jesus, You are King, we are Your subjects. You lead us.*

Palm Sunday traditions vary throughout history and throughout the world, but one practice in various places is for the children of the congregation to process into the sanctuary at the beginning of worship singing and carrying palm branches. This captures the movement and procession of Jesus into the holy city, as He was carried along and "enthroned" on the praises of Israel. The liturgical color for Palm Sunday remains the royal purple of Lent.

Maundy Thursday

On Maundy Thursday, we remember the night on which Jesus ate with His disciples at the Passover table, instituted the Lord's Supper, washed His disciples' feet, and prayed in the Garden of Gethsemane. Maundy Thursday is so called because of the saying of Jesus to His disciples in John 13:34, "A new commandment I give to you, that you love one another." In Latin the first words of this verse are *Mandatum novum*, thus the word *mandatum* has become, in English, "Maundy."

Because the institution of the Lord's Supper is at the center of these events, the Maundy Thursday service traditionally includes communion. Since, however, every Lord's Day worship service is in effect a celebration of the events of Maundy Thursday, this is not absolutely necessary. It is best to hold the complete covenant renewal liturgy at regular times on the Lord's Day when the whole congregation is expected to be present. If a special service on this day is held at a time where the majority of the congregation cannot be present, it would be best not to include communion but to make the "mandate" of love the central focus of the service. If communion is to be included, the entire liturgical progression of confession of sins, consecration by the Word, and communion should be followed.

Another Maundy Thursday practice in various quarters is the incorporation of a foot-washing service, where the members of the congregation literally wash each other's feet as Jesus did for the disciples. Because the washing of a guest's feet is no longer a cultural or practical necessity, this is an odd proposition for most modern people. Furthermore, it is likely that the cleansing ritual in the upper room had ties to the cleansings necessary under the Old Covenant. The ground is cursed, after all, and people needed some ritual and symbolic cleansing after they come in contact with it. But that old world has passed away, and Jesus has cleansed the world. The ground and the dirt no longer make us "unclean" in any ritual or symbolic sense.

Some thought could be given, though, to what a modern parallel to foot-washing would be, and how we could perform acts of kindness for each other which are menial and which we might be tempted to think are "beneath us." This is the central point of the "mandate" we are given on Maundy Thursday.

Good Friday

On Good Friday, we meditate on the day on which Jesus was betrayed, arrested, tried, scourged, mocked, condemned, crucified, and laid in a tomb. Because of the grave and serious nature of these events, our worship and reflection are subdued and sober, and yet not entirely without joy. Remember that we do not go through these days of worship and remembrance playing make-believe as if it is our first time hearing of these events and acting as if we do not know how things turn out in the end. Even on Good Friday, we must hold before us the truth and power of the resurrection. On this day we are rejoicing in the great victory of the King who is presently not on a cross, nor in a grave, but who has been exalted over all things and currently reigns from His throne.

It is tempting to turn the Good Friday service into a very dark, morose funeral for Jesus. Churches can go out of the way to cut the lights, shroud all of the sanctuary furniture and fixtures in black, and to insist that no one talk or greet each other before or after worship. The intent is sincere, but the effect is to teach something that is not true, and that is the idea that the cross of Jesus is an occasion for great mourning and sorrow. Certainly that was the case for the women and the disciples in the story who did not fully understand what was coming, but that is not the case for us.

Worship on Good Friday must certainly have a sense of gravity, largely because of the guilt of our own sin that made the cross a necessity. However, we do not wallow in our sin, nor do we dwell on the graphic and gory details of the practice of crucifixion—which the gospel writers do not even go into. We exult in the power and the majesty and might of our King who by the cross secured so great a victory, and rejoicing in Him, we commit ourselves to take up our cross, to die to our sins, and to live cruciform lives ourselves.

For worship on this day it is appropriate to simply remove all the ordinary-colored paraments from the sanctuary. No other funereal decoration is necessary. It is good to read through the crucifix-ion account in its entirety, to sing hymns about the passion and suffering of Jesus, to reflect on what Jesus accomplished on the cross, and then to end the service with a exuberant song of victory and a joyful benediction, reminding ourselves of the crushed head of the Serpent and of the great things we are about to celebrate on Easter morning.

A BRIEF ORDER FOR
HOLY WEEK DEVOTION

Opening Psalm
The family may begin by singing one of the following psalms: 8, 22, 23, 24, 27, 32, 56, 64, 69, 143

Opening Prayer
Leader: Let us pray.

Palm Sunday

All: **O Lord Jesus Christ, who as on this day entered the rebellious city where You were to die: enter into our hearts, we pray, and subdue them wholly to You. And as Your faithful disciples blessed Your coming and spread their garments in the way, covering it with palm branches, make us ready to lay at Your feet all that we have and are, and to** bless You, O You who comes in the name of the Lord. And grant that after having confessed and worshiped You upon earth, we may be among the number of those who shall hail Your eternal triumph and bear in our hands the palms of victory, when every knee bows before You, and every tongue confess that You are Lord, to the glory of God the Father. Amen!

Monday

All: Almighty God, whose most dear son went not up to joy, but first he suffered pain, and entered not into glory before He was crucified; mercifully grant that we, walking in the way of the cross, may find it none other than the way of life and peace; through Your son Jesus Christ our Lord. Amen!

Tuesday

All: O Lord God, whose blessed son, our savior, gave his back to the smiters and did not hide his face from shame; grant us grace to take joyfully the suffering of the present time, in full assurance of the glory that shall be revealed; through Your son Jesus Christ our Lord. Amen!

Wednesday

All: Assist us mercifully with Your self, O Lord God of our salvation; that we may enter with joy upon the meditation of these mighty acts, by which You have given us life and immortality; through Jesus Christ our Lord. Amen!

Maundy Thursday

All: Almighty Father, whose beloved son, on the night before he suffered, instituted the sacrament of his body and blood; mercifully grant that we may thankfully receive it in remembrance of Him, who in these mysteries gives us a pledge of life eternal; Your son Jesus Christ our Lord, who now lives and reigns with You and the Holy Ghost forever; one God, world without end. Amen!

Good Friday

All: O Lord Jesus Christ, who for our sakes suffered death on the cross; help us to bear about with us Your dying, and, in our living, to show forth Your life. Looking on You whom we have pierced, we would mourn for our sins with unfeigned sorrow; we would learn from You to forgive, with You to suffer, and in You to overcome. Lamb of God, who takes away the sins of the world, have mercy upon us. Lamb of God, who takes away the sins of the world, grant us Your peace. Lord, we pray, in Your great mercy, remember us when You perfect your kingdom. Amen!

Saturday

All: O God, whose only-begotten son followed the way of faith and duty even to the crown of thorns and the cross; give us grace that we may learn the harder lessons of our faith. And so endue us with power from on high, that, taking up our cross and following our savior in His patience and humility, we may enter into the fellowship of His sufferings, and come at last to dwell with Him in His eternal kingdom; through Jesus Christ our Lord. Amen!

Scripture Readings
Palm Sunday
Zech. 9:9–14; Mal. 3:1–12; Mk. 11:1–11; Ps. 8 & 62

Monday
1 Cor. 1:18–25; Mk. 11:12–24; Ps. 6

Tuesday
Zech. 13; Mt. 21:23–32; Ps. 31

Wednesday
Gen. 37:13–28; Mt. 26:1–16; Ps. 55

Maundy Thursday
Ex. 24:1–11; Lk. 22:1–30; Ps. 64

Good Friday
Gen. 22:1–19; Jn. 19; Heb. 10:1–25; Ps. 69

Saturday
Hos. 6:1–6; Mk. 15:42–47; 1 Pet. 3:7–22; Ps. 30

Hymn
Select one of the following hymns for Palm Sunday:

- All Glory, Laud, and Honor
- O Lord, How Shall I Meet Thee

Hymns for the Remainder of the Week :

- A Lamb Goes Uncomplaining Forth
- Ah, Holy Jesus, How Hast Thou Offended
- How Sweet and Awful Is the Place
- Jesus, Thy Blood and Righteousness
- Jesus! What a Friend for Sinners!
- Let Thy Blood in Mercy Poured

- O Lamb of God Most Holy
- O Sacred Head, Now Wounded
- O the Deep, Deep Love of Jesus
- Stricken, Smitten, and Afflicted
- Through Every Age, Eternal God
- When I Survey the Wondrous Cross

Prayer Requests & Closing Prayer
Family members may make specific prayer requests, after which the entire family can pray.

Leader: Grace, mercy, and peace from God the Father, Son, and Holy Ghost, be with us now and forever.

All: Amen!

Easter

The Lord is risen indeed!
—Luke 24:34

The Easter season is a festival season wherein we celebrate the Resurrection of our Lord Jesus Christ. Just as we observe not just one Christmas day, but an entire twelve-day season of Christmas, so our celebration at Easter is not contained to one Sunday only, but rather, a full forty-nine day period from Resurrection Sunday to Pentecost. These forty-nine days of Eastertide parallel the forty days that Jesus spent with his apostles after his resurrection plus the nine days that the apostles waited in Jerusalem after His ascension. During these days of the liturgical year the Church rejoices in and reflects upon the significance of the resurrection and how this event has reshaped the cosmos. We contemplate the way that the old order was buried with Jesus in his death, and how the new heavens and the new earth have been ushered in with His resurrection. The world is a different place after the resurrection of Jesus. During Eastertide, we rest in the realities of this new world.

This season is a joyful celebration with a particular emphasis on the victory of Jesus over the grave. Because Jesus has gone into the grave, and come out the other side, we are no longer slaves to death. For those who are united by baptism to the death, burial and resurrection of Jesus, death is only the gateway to more life.

At various times throughout Church history, Easter Sunday has been the preferred day for baptisms, especially for those new converts who had spent the Lenten season being catechized in the Christian faith. Other Easter Season traditions include the decoration of eggs and various games involving eggs, which from antiquity have been viewed by the church as a symbol of new life. It is also customary to serve the best meats, drinks, and chocolates over these feast days, enjoying the fullness of the creation that Jesus has redeemed.

On this Sunday, and throughout Eastertide, we change the sanctuary color to radiant white, which signifies the glory of the resurrection.

A BRIEF ORDER FOR
EASTER FAMILY DEVOTIONS

Opening Psalm
The family may begin by singing one of the following psalms: 57, 93, 98, 111, 113, 114, 118

Opening Prayer
Leader: Let us pray.

All: Jesus, brightness of God's glory and image of His being, whom death could not conquer nor tomb imprison; as You have shared in our mortality, help us to share in Your immortal triumph. Let no shadow of the grave frighten us and no fear of darkness turn our hearts from You. Reveal Yourself to us as the first and the last, the living one, our immortal Savior and Lord. Amen!

Scripture Readings
Ex. 12:1-28, 40-42; Lk. 24:13-49; Ex. 15:1-18; Ps. 115

Hymn
Select one of the following hymns:

- Christ Jesus Lay in Death's Strong Bands
- Christ the Lord Is Ris'n Today

- Hail Thee, Festival Day!
- Now Let the Vault of Heaven Resound
- O Paschal Feast, What Joy Is Thine
- That Easter Day with Joy Was Bright
- The Strife Is O'er
- Thou Hallowed Chosen Morn of Praise

Prayer Requests & Closing Prayer
Family members may make specific prayer requests, after which the entire family can pray.

Leader: May the God of peace, who brought again from the dead our Lord Jesus, that great shepherd of the sheep, through the blood of the everlasting covenant, make us perfect in every good work to do His will, working in us that which is well-pleasing in His sight; through Jesus Christ, to whom be glory for ever and ever.

All: Amen!

Ascension

This man, after he had offered one sacrifice for sins forever, sat down at the right hand of God.
—Hebrews 10:12

The Forgotten Holiday

The Scriptures tells us that for forty days after His resurrection, Jesus walked with and taught His disciples on earth and afterward ascended into the heavens to take His place at the Father's right hand.

Ascension Day is marked in many places throughout Christendom by special feasts and worship services. In an explicitly Christian society, businesses and schools would close, and everyone would stop and praise King Jesus for his rule over the earth.

On this day we celebrate that occasion when Jesus publicly displayed his ascent into the heavenlies and was received up into a cloud, leaving his people with a sense of his continuing presence and rule. In witnessing this, they knew that he had not really gone far away. The apostles did not think of heaven as some far off place at the outer edge of the universe that we could get to if we had a space ship to take us that far. They understood that heaven and earth overlap—that there are all kinds of heavenly spiritual things around us and above us that we cannot see with our eyes, but are really there.

They understood what the cloud was. Throughout the Bible clouds both represent and hide God's heavenly glory. Think of the cloud that led Israel in the wilderness, the glory cloud that filled the tabernacle and temple, or the bright cloud that enveloped Moses and Elijah on the Mount of Transfiguration. Over and over throughout the scriptures people hear God's voice speaking from a cloud. If God's throne room were an iceberg, the glory cloud would be just a tip of that iceberg.

Surely Psalm 68 crossed the minds of the Apostles that day: "Sing to God, sing praise to his name, extol him who rides on the clouds—his name is Yahweh—rejoice before him." When Jesus was taken up into the cloud, there was no doubt in the apostles' minds where Jesus was going or who he was.

Jesus, the victorious God-man, entered heaven to be our representative before the Father. Everything that Jesus did, He did for us and with us. Jesus' ascension comforts the church because his ascension is our ascension. Now one of us, the man Jesus, is in heaven. Because He is accepted and welcomed there, we are accepted and welcomed there. Because His work is accepted there, our work is accepted there. As He is seated in the heavenlies, so now, as Ephesians 2:6 says, we are seated in the heavenlies.

Now stationed at the Father's right hand, He answers every charge the accuser brings against us. We know that because of this there is always forgiveness. We know that our prayers always reach the Father's ears, and we will always get the Father's attention, having our prayers answered lovingly with heavenly wisdom and power.

Jesus' ascension guarantees the Church victory in her mission. Jesus not only acts as an intercessor for us, but He also brings his own prayers. The Father tells the son in Psalm 2, "Ask of me and I will give you the nations as an inheritance." Jesus responds to that invitation and asks His Father for the nations.

In the ascension we see that Jesus is King. He rules over heaven and earth, and He does it with our interests in mind. Though mankind was at one time cut off from fellowship with the Father, exiled from the garden sanctuary, and held at arm's length through the various zones of holiness at the tabernacle, now Jesus' ascension has opened heaven itself to us. Now we have access with Jesus into not just an earthly sanctuary divided by curtains and coverings. In worship we ascend into the heavenlies and join in the heavenly worship. We can now truly enter his gates with thanksgiving and his courts with praise.

Ascension Devotional Aids

You might celebrate Ascension Day by listening to one of the following musical reflections on the ascension.

Bach's *Ascension Oratorio*
Praise, My Soul, the King of Heaven
Psalm 47

A BRIEF ORDER FOR
ASCENSION FAMILY DEVOTIONS

Opening Psalm
The family may begin by singing one of the following psalms: 15, 24, 27, 47, 96, 97

Opening Prayer

Leader: Let us pray.

All: Almighty God, whose blessed son our savior Jesus Christ ascended far above all heav-

ens that he might fill all things: mercifully give us faith to perceive that, according to his promise, he abides with his church on earth, even to the end of the ages; through Jesus Christ our Lord, who lives and reigns with you and the Holy Ghost, one God, in glory everlasting. Amen!

Scripture Readings
Dan. 7:9-14; Heb. 1; Acts 1:1-11; Ps. 68

Hymn
Select one of the following hymns:

- On Christ's Ascension I Now Build
- Rejoice! the Lord Is King
- See, the Conqueror Mounts in Triumph

Prayer Requests & Closing Prayer
Family members may make specific prayer requests, after which the entire family can pray.

Leader: The almighty and merciful God, the Father, the Son, and the Holy Spirit, bless us and keep us.

All: Amen!

Pentecost

Because you are sons, God sent the Spirit of His Son
into your hearts, who calls, "Abba! Father!"
—Galatians 4:6

Words of Fire

On the fiftieth day after Easter we celebrate the feast of Pentecost, the day on which the prophecy of Joel was fulfilled as the Holy Spirit was poured out upon the church, anointing her and equipping her to complete her mission in the world. Just as God breathed life into Adam's nostrils, making him a living soul, so on the day of Pentecost God breathed life into the Church and filled her with that same life-giving Spirit.

As the Spirit hovered over the waters of the first creation, and as the wind blew back the waters of the flood and the waters of the Red Sea, just as the Spirit hovered over the waters of Jesus' baptism as a dove, so the rushing mighty wind of the Spirit blew over the waters of thousands of baptisms on Pentecost.

This day is also known as Whitsunday throughout parts of the English-speaking world. *Whit* or *wit* is an old English word for "spirit." *Wit* today, of course, means "clever speech." These two definitions are not unconnected.

Certainly the apostles were filled with both the Spirit and the gift of clever speech as they preached in tongues to the people gathered in Jerusalem. This is a day to not only give thanks for the outpouring of the Holy Spirit, but also for the gift of language by which we communicate the gospel, breathing out words of life to a dead world.

Red is the liturgical color of Pentecost since it reminds us of the tongues of fire that rested on the heads of the apostles. We remember also that we are the new altar that is lit by the fire of the Holy Spirit. One custom is for the entire congregation to wear red on Pentecost to reflect this.

Except for Trinity Sunday and All Saints' Day, the Sundays between Pentecost and Advent are generally referred to as "Sundays after Pentecost" and mark the weeks of "ordinary time" on the church calendar. Our sanctuary colors return to the growing green as we focus on the growth of the church and the outworking of the kingdom until we cycle back to the purple of Advent, where we once again look forward to the future coming of King Jesus.

A BRIEF ORDER FOR
PENTECOST FAMILY DEVOTIONS

Opening Psalm
The family may begin by singing one of the following Psalms: 18, 48, 68, 104, 112, 145

Opening Prayer
Leader: Let us pray.

All: O God, who sanctifies Your catholic church in every race and nation; send throughout the whole world the gift of the Holy Spirit, that the work done by His power at the first preaching of the gospel may now be suffused among all nations; through Jesus Christ our Lord. Amen!

Scripture Readings
Is. 55; Joel 2:21-32; Acts 2:1-11; Ps. 145

Hymn
Select one of the following hymns:
- Come Down, O Love Divine
- Come, Holy Ghost, Our Souls Inspire
- Love Divine, All Loves Excelling
- O Heav'nly Word, Eternal Light
- We Now Implore God the Holy Ghost

Prayer Requests & Closing Prayer

*Family members may make specific prayer requests,
after which the entire family can pray.*

Leader: May the God of peace sanctify us wholly
and preserve us blameless until the coming
of our Lord Jesus Christ.

All: Amen!

Trinity

Holy, holy, holy, Lord God Almighty,
Who was and is and is to come!
—Revelation 4:8

Community of the Trinity

On the Sunday after Pentecost the church places special emphasis on the doctrine of the Trinity. Through songs, readings, prayers and sermons we reinforce the foundational Christian teaching that the God of creation has eternally existed in a covenant of three persons: the Father, the Son and the Holy Spirit. By returning each year to spend one Sunday on this doctrine, we remember that the Trinity is not an esoteric piece of theological trivia but rather is the very definition of God. The one and only, true and living God has revealed Himself to us as a Trinity of three persons in community. We then understand that if we are to reflect His image then we, too, must live in community with the Body of Christ.

On this day we return to "growing green" for the sanctuary as we enter the long ordinary season of growth and maturation.

A BRIEF ORDER FOR
TRINITY FAMILY DEVOTIONS

Opening Psalm
The family may begin by singing one of the following psalms: 29, 139

Opening Prayer
Leader: Let us pray.

All: **Almighty and everlasting God, who has given us, your servants, grace, by the confession of a true faith to acknowledge the glory of the eternal Trinity, and in the power of the Divine Majesty to worship the Unity; we pray that You would keep us steadfast in this faith and evermore defend us from all adversities, who lives and reigns, one God, world without end. Amen!**

Scripture Readings
Is. 6:1-8; 63:7-19; Jn. 3:1-21; Rom. 5:1-5; Rev. 4

Hymn
Select one of the following hymns:

• Holy, Holy, Holy
• St. Patrick's Breastplate (The Lorica)

Prayer Requests & Closing Prayer
Family members may make specific prayer requests, after which the entire family can pray.

Leader: The almighty and merciful God, the Father, the Son, and the Holy Spirit, bless us and keep us.

All: Amen!

All Saints

You have made them kings and priests to our God.
And they shall reign forever and ever.
—Revelation 5:10; 22:5

To Follow in Their Train

In the early church it was common to commemorate the Christian martyrs with a feast day of giving thanks for their faith and sacrifice. However, by the fourth century the list of martyrs had grown so long that the church could no longer dedicate an entire day to every one of them. Thus, the practice of celebrating one common feast day in memory of all the martyrs and departed saints was born.

On the closest Sunday to November 1, the Church remembers that she stands at the end of a long line of faithful men and women throughout the centuries who each preserved the faith in their own day. The church gives thanks for their lives, for their examples and for their service and sacrifices for the Lord Jesus. We remember our own fathers and mothers in the faith, and also give thanks for the lives of friends and loved ones who have passed. As they continually worship before the throne of God, we remember that each Lord's day our voices are joining their songs of praise and we worship with them in the Spirit. We reflect on the fact that we are truly surrounded by a great cloud of witnesses.

All Hallows, Reformed

The night before All Saints Day is All Saints Eve or All Hallows Eve, commonly shortened to "Hallowe'en." While this day has been secularized and commercialized, Hallowe'en is more properly understood as a celebration of the saints' triumph over Satan. The tradition of dressing in ridiculous parodies of Satan's hosts mocks our accuser for his failure to defeat the saints and reminds him that even in our deaths we have the victory in Jesus. Children may participate by dressing up and openly exposing the powerlessness of the darkness over us.

It is common in Reformed and Lutheran churches at this same time to remember the beginning of the Reformation on October 31, 1517. These two commemorations—All Saints' and Reformation Day—need not to be viewed as if they were in competition with each other. Martin Luther posted his theses at the church on Hallowe'en because he knew many would be coming to church for All Saints' Day and see his proclamation there. In our All Saints' Day activities and prayers we give thanks for all of the great lights of Church history, including Martin Luther, John Calvin, John Knox, and all the other heroes of the Reformation.

A BRIEF ORDER FOR
ALL SAINTS' FAMILY DEVOTIONS

Opening Psalm
The family may begin by singing one of the following psalms: 24, 34, 149

Opening Prayer
Leader: Let us pray.

All: **We give thanks to You, O Lord, for all Your saints and servants, who have done justly, loved mercy, and walked humbly with their God. For all the high and holy ones, who have wrought wonders and been shining lights in the world, we thank You. For all the meek and lowly ones, who have earnestly sought You in darkness and held fast their faith in trial, and done good to all men as they had opportunity, we thank You. Especially for those men and women whom**

we have known and loved, who by their patient obedience and self-denial, steadfast hope and helpfulness in trouble, have shown the same mind that was in Christ Jesus, we bless Your holy name. As they have comforted and upheld our souls, grant us grace to follow in their steps, and at last to share with them in the inheritance of the saints in light; through Jesus Christ our savior. Amen!

Scripture Readings

Is. 25: 1-9; Mt. 5:12; Rev. 7:9-17

Hymn

Select one of the following hymns:

- For All the Saints
- How Firm a Foundation
- I Love Thy Kingdom, Lord
- Jesus, with Thy Church Abide
- O God of Earth and Altar
- The Church's One Foundation
- The Son of God Goes Forth to War

Prayer Requests & Closing Prayer

Family members may make specific prayer requests, after which the entire family can pray.

Leader: May the God of peace sanctify us wholly, and preserve us blameless unto the coming of our Lord Jesus Christ.

All: Amen!

The Christian
Discipline of
Festivity

What are the most important Christian disciplines? I recently did a search online for various books on the subject to see how various pastors and authors would answer that question. Among the results I found references to some of the basic disciplines we would all expect, such as prayer, Bible study, tithing, worship, and evangelism. But I also found on these lists such disciplines as "solitude," "silence," "quiet," "mindfulness," "meditation," "simplicity," "frugality," and "journaling." Of course, given the number of times it comes up in the Psalms who could deny the value of meditation? But "journaling?" Where do I go in the Bible to learn how to "journal" in a way that pleases God?

There seems to be a popular assumption that the Christian faith is practiced most purely in an environment of solitude, silence, and contemplation. This list of "disciplines" certainly reflects that assumption. It is as if the Christian faith can be faithfully practiced entirely by yourself, in total silence, in the dark, far removed from other people. We seem to think that one can perform everything that it means to be a Christian in one's head, because the Christian faith, after all, is mostly about thinking certain things and believing certain things.

However, if silence and solitude are the purest expressions of the Christian faith, then why do we need the Church or Word or Sacraments? Why would we ever need other people? Indeed, that is exactly the point. If you scratch the surface of many popular Christian writers and their works, you find underneath a general antipathy for the physical institution of the Church. The purest expression of the Christian faith, in so much writing and preaching, is mostly found in the realm of the individual, the internal, the subjective, and the private.

Yet the reality is that the Church of the Lord Jesus Christ is the complete opposite of all that. The church is communal, external, deals in objective realities, and she carries out her work in public. She is not quiet, she is loud, and if she is being faithful, her presence is heard and felt and known. Quiet and rest and meditation are not objectionable, but we should want to run in the opposite direction when we hear those things heralded as the best or purest expressions of the Christian faith. The Christian faith is most fully expressed and modeled not when we are isolated and alone. The Christian faith is best expressed when we are together, and it is on display in the things we do when we are together. Therefore, in any discussion of basic Christian disciplines, we ought to include the Christian duties of festivity, of rejoicing, of making merry, of feasting.

When God created man, His first covenant with him was an arrangement involving food. The first command was "Eat this, not that." That covenant pointed to a fundamental built-in characteristic of man. Man eats. God created man as a being who is contingent on food. Man must eat to live and if he stops eating, he will die. God could have created mankind with any manner of faculties for gaining nourishment. We might have been created with green skin to soak up our energy from the sun, like the plants. God could have designed things in such a way that we could get all that we need from the air, or maybe we could filter plankton from the water we drink. But He did not do any of that. The Lord designed man's body to eat dead plants and dead animals for its strength and nourishment. Ordinarily, everything we eat is dead. We eat dead chickens and cows and fish, and from these dead animals, God amazingly, miraculously gives us life.

Whether you give Him thanks or not, whether you acknowledge it or not, when you eat, the Holy

Spirit is giving you life from dead things. Somehow, He turns a chicken nugget into an arm, and macaroni into a lung. Furthermore, these things we eat are the fruits of our labor – either picked from a garden, or orchard, or harvested from a field, or from animals that are either hunted or husbanded. God feeds us through the work and industry of man tending to plants and animals.

This God who feeds us this way gives us not just one thing to eat, and not just one thing to drink. Our only food is not gray, room-temperature oatmeal, but in God's creation we have discovered an abundant plethora of good things to eat. We have so many options that we are often crippled by the host of choices when we try to decide what to have for supper. God has poured out such a diversity of plant and animal life on this planet that no one can accuse him of being stingy or miserly with His good gifts. There are thousands upon thousands of varieties of fruits and vegetables in the world. There are something like 7500 varieties of apples. There are over 4000 varieties of potato. How many can you name? Add to this all of the various animals that are good for food. God has spread a great buffet before man, not just for man's nourishment, but for man's pleasure.

After Adam's fall, God continued to feed man, but He warned him that it is going to be harder work to get food out of the ground. Adam's sons brought the offerings of their herds and fields to the Lord, acknowledging that the Lord is the one who gave these things. After the flood, when God made sure to preserve all those good meats on Noah's barge, God gave new instructions regarding food. He said "every living thing shall be food for you, but don't eat flesh with its life. Don't eat its blood." God required His people to have a different attitude about food. Everything we do is under God's authority and we do it God's way. We eat animals, but we don't eat like animals, we eat like men. We are not to eat our meat bloody and raw, but we must drain the blood, and this directive also implies the necessity of cooking, which brings additional dimensions to the character and flavor of our food. Noah went out from there and planted a vineyard and enjoyed the wine that God provided to gladden his heart (Psalm 104:15).

Moving forward in Bible history, God cut his covenant with Abraham with animal sacrifices. Melchizedek brought bread and wine so that when Abraham brings his tithe, we see that worship and obedience and good food and drink go together. Eating together with God and eating together before God is a demonstration of our unity, friendship, and agreement. You don't typically eat with people you don't like. We do not usually call up our worst enemy and invite them to scowl at us over a cheeseburger. Typically, eating together moves us toward unity. Eating together binds us together. If we do eat together with our enemy, it typically means that we are working toward reconciliation.

Later in Genesis, Abraham and Sarah entertain the angelic messengers of the Lord in the form of three visitors. Abraham tells Sarah to make some bread—three measures of fine meal, refined flour— which is enough flour for sixty loaves of bread. Abraham kills a calf, and they end up with a feast of beef, a mountain of bread, milk, and butter. Abraham and Sarah prepare this elaborate meal because they walk with a God who is not stingy with His blessings. How do you respond to a God like this, but with extravagance? You feast before the Lord, with His messengers with more bread and beef and dairy than three men could eat in a week.

There are many other significant scenes in Genesis surrounding food, like Jacob and Esau, and a bowl of lentils. Later we find Jacob and Isaac sharing some roasted goat. Food is at the center of agreements and covenants. God sovereignly puts Joseph in a position to save the world, by feeding the world. All the world is starving, but Egypt has grain. Why does Egypt have grain? Because God blessed Egypt with Joseph who is a deliverer, a savior, rejected by his brothers, put to death, resurrected as a king, who feeds the world. (Whom does that sound like?)

It is good food that God promises to Israel when he frees them from slavery in Egypt. Through Moses, He promises them a land flowing with milk and honey. Notice the emphasis on things that are fat and sweet: milk and honey. If He had advertised Canaan as a land flowing with broccoli and radishes, nobody would have left Egypt. No one is going to go kill a giant just so they can eat a big bowl of rabbit food. But you will kill a giant for a gooey cinnamon roll. When the psalmist sings "taste and see that the Lord is good" and "your words are sweeter than honey," there is a close connection between the good words and laws God gives His people, and the good food He gives his people. Those aren't just word-pictures for them to meditate on because super-spiritual people have no idea what sweet stuff is like. They know the Word of God is sweet because they have eaten the honey God gave them, and drank the wine He provided.

God delivers Israel from Egypt in the midst of a ritual meal, the Passover, and by properly keeping the feast, their families are spared. One of the ways Israel is identified is by the food they eat and how they eat it, in contrast to the Egyptians who do not keep the feast. With the Passover, those who participate in the feast have life. If you decide to ignore the feast that God has ordained, then death will visit your house. This feast was one that was to be kept by Israel throughout the generations to commemorate God's love and deliverance of His people.

Passover becomes one of several feasts God puts on the calendar. The Lord gives them six feasts, seven if you count Purim which came during Esther's time, and among these only one fast day. They have seven annual feasts together, along with the Sabbath which was a weekly feast, and all the other feasts of the new moon and the harvests. All these feasts were prescribed by God, so that Israel would be known among the nations of the world not as a nation that starved, not as a nation that did without and were deprived, but as a nation that was so blessed that they came together often for these amazing, lavish celebrations full of good things to eat.

In Deuteronomy 14:22-29 the Lord prescribes the order for one of those feasts, the Feast of Tabernacles. In order to commemorate their time in the wilderness, back when they did not have a settled home, every year they were to construct makeshift booths out of branches and limbs and live in them for seven days. This would have been something like a weeklong family campout. Imagine how much the children would look forward to something like that every year. The Lord commanded them that in preparation for this festival that they were to take a tithe of the increase of their grain and wine and oil and herds and make an offering and eat at the tabernacle or temple. But if it was too far for them to travel, or if that offering is too big for them to take with them, they were to exchange that offering for money, take the money and throw a party. God says "buy whatever you want." Go out and acquire whatever your heart desires, be it oxen, sheep, wine, beer. Whatever you like buy it, eat it, and rejoice before the Lord your God. Also, bring in the stranger, the one without the inheritance, the fatherless, the widow and eat with them too.

This was all a commandment of God. None of this was optional. He does not say, "If you feel like it, throw a party." Or "If you are up to it, have a feast." No, He says, "I want you to take a tenth of your increase and go nuts with it." They were to go buy the best food and the best drink and make a really big deal about all of it. To think of this in our own terms, how much did you make last year? What is ten percent of that? What kind of party could you throw with that? Imagine if you are not the only one throwing that kind of party but that everyone around you is as well. We simply do not have the capacity to even imagine that kind of festivity. We think it is a really big deal when a whole family shares a turkey. "Look at you! You served both a ham and a turkey for Christmas! Look at Mr. Moneybags over here." As far as the Bible is concerned, when it comes to feasting, there is nothing that we can do that God would consider "overdoing it." In fact, the phrase "overdoing it" doesn't seem to be in His vocabulary.

When Jesus comes, He does the same sort of thing. Jesus doesn't come to wander around in solitude and quiet. He is not off in a corner, meditating all the time. Jesus works His first miracle at a wedding feast, and he makes wine, not just any wine but the good stuff, and how much? He makes six water pots – around twenty gallons each – which comes to 120 gallons of wine. If someone shows up to your house with 120 gallons of wine, you might say "the party is on."

As Jesus moves through his ministry, He heals and teaches during the day, but in the evenings, we find Him in homes around the tables of people of all backgrounds and reputations. There He eats with people, communes with them, loves them across the table. Someone once said that the gospel of Luke is just one big progressive dinner, because the scene moves from table to table. Just as Jesus made more wine than was necessary, when He feeds five thousand and then four thousand, there's so much bread and fish left over that they have to pick it up in baskets. There is a bounty and abundance of food whenever Jesus works a miracle. It looks excessive and extravagant, but Jesus does this because His Father is not stingy with His blessings; He isn't miserly. He is not selfish and He does not want His people to be selfish either.

The people who follow Jesus pick up on His extravagance and imitate it. Mary lavishes a pound of very costly oil on Jesus. She gives not just a dab, not just a squirt, but a pound of perfume. John wrote, "the house was filled with the fragrance." I bet it was. Not only the house, but down the street, and the whole neighborhood would have smelled it. Judas was sitting over there in the corner complaining about the waste, but Judas only reveals himself for who he is. He is the miser. He is stealing. He is selfish. The people who follow Jesus, follow the Savior's extravagance. When they want to demonstrate their love, they overdo it. If someone is not asking "can we really afford this?" then you haven't quite done enough.

The point of this quick journey through the Scriptures is that putting good food on the table and getting people around to enjoy it is as much a Christian discipline as prayer or tithing or Bible study. This is something that God's people have always made a point of doing. When we do this, we are following Jesus. It is around the table, sharing good food and drink where we manifest the Christian faith in ways that cannot be done if we are all off by ourselves in quiet and solitude. If solitude, quiet, and journaling is your paradigm of the Christian faith, I want to help shift that a little bit, just bump it, so that you can see that we were not created to be alone, or even all alone with God, but that we were created to enjoy union and communion with Jesus and His people. The Christian calendar of feast days gives us all kinds of opportunities and occasions for us to exercise this discipline of feasting together.

It is no secret that our enemy, Satan, really does not like this feasting thing. We are easier targets when we are by ourselves. When we get together to have lots of fun, it is harder for Satan to make the world believe we are a bunch of lifeless fuddy duds. When we gather to give God thanks for good food and wine, we are a formidable army of gratitude, and Satan hates that. So he's always done his best to attack joyous feasting among God's people to stir up conflict and opposition to it.

There were those who accused Jesus of not fasting enough, of being a glutton and a drunkard. They didn't like how much Jesus ate, and they didn't like who he ate with. If Jesus was attacked at the table, you can bet his church is too. The first internal controversy in the church that we read about was a matter of whose widowed grandmothers were getting fed and whose were left out. Many in the church were later scandalized by the fact that as the church spread into the world that Christians would have to share the table with Gentiles, and maybe even eat the things that Gentiles ate. The first church council in Acts 15 convened and addressed this issue. Later Paul had to work on the same set of concerns with the church in Corinth and answered the questions, "What can we eat? What's forbidden?" Their food problems all overflowed onto their practices at the Lord's table. What happens at the banquet table and the dinner table is important; these are not small questions.

If Satan has his way, our tables are not going to be places of unity and communion, but places of anxiety, and strife, and contention. The table of friendship becomes a battleground instead. Americans especially have developed an immense sense of anxiety when it comes to their food. We are so rich, and have so much food, that we can afford to be really really picky and really anxious about what we eat and where it comes from. We are grieved about whether the chicken had a moment of panic before she was turned into nuggets. We wonder what does our food have in it? There is a popular fanaticism about food that develops into forms of neurosis and idolatry. Food is no longer viewed as a source of God's goodness and blessing and life toward us. It is feared, it is dangerous, it is corrupt. Our primary impulse regarding food turns from gratitude to disgust. We begin to act as if apart from God, we can depend entirely on eating the perfectly pure food, and are completely in control of our health and well-being by eating the right things. We forget that it is God who sanctifies all food, and turns all food into life. "For every creature of God is good, and nothing to be refused, if it be received with thanksgiving: For it is sanctified by the word of God and prayer" (1 Timothy 4:4-5).

What happens if we ignore all of this and develop a conviction that we are only going to eat organic, free range, cruelty free, fair-trade brussels sprouts? What if we also become convinced in our own minds that everyone who does not join us in this only acceptable perfectly healthy holy new diet is a Philistine? You are likely to find yourself very alone, and in a hurry. You are not going to be happy joining anyone else's table and no one will want to join yours, except out of pity. You have taken the table that God has given to hold a bounty of His goodness and you have turned it into a place of divisiveness, pettiness, and obnoxiousness.

Of course, there are some folks who really do have physical issues that prevent them from eating certain things. There are some foods they may need to stay away from for medical reasons. You are not feasting joyfully if you know that in twenty minutes you are going to break out in welts. But outside of legitimate health issues, we must avoid making up anxieties about food. We must not create problems for ourselves where there are none and we must avoid playing into our materialistic culture's messianic view of diets. If you do have a legitimate health issue in your home, you work diligently to compensate in other ways so as not to telegraph tension and fear all over the place. Make every effort to not allow food anxiety to dampen the real joy of how God intends for us to enjoy food and feasting.

We must always ask ourselves whose agenda we are following with our attitudes toward food? Are our beliefs and practices consistent with the God who is worshipped when the saints break out sixty loaves of bread and 120 gallons of wine? Or are we more consistent with Satan who wants nothing more than to disrupt the feasts and make us feel really guilty for eating?

All of this Biblical emphasis on feasting and festivity underscores why we should to follow the Christian calendar. We need to be reminded at different parts of the year it is time to stop and rejoice. If we do not have set feast days, then we are going to merely stampede right through life, working and plowing, never resting. Prescribed feast days remind us that whether we feel like it or not, whether we are up to it or not, we need to lay aside our sorrows, lay aside our doubt and anxiety and worry, and rest in the love of Jesus by roasting a turkey, smoking a brisket, pouring a glass of wine, and cutting a big slice of cake.

When we live this way, putting a regular, deliberate emphasis on rejoicing together around good food and drink, this is glory. This is attractive. This is a city on a hill. The call of the gospel is to come sit down and eat with Jesus. Somewhere we got this idea that the way the Gospel spread throughout the ancient world was by people standing on the street corner screaming about it. But that's not even close to the reality. Jesus taught his disciples publicly and engaged inquirers. Peter preached in the temple. Paul went to the synagogues and the places of pagan worship. These were all places where people were already gathered for conversation. But where did they always end up? When evening came, they were in someone's home, around their table.

Remembering what we read above in Deuteronomy, about the Feast of Tabernacles, God's command was explicit. The point of all of this is not merely that you have a good time by yourself with your inner circle of friends, but that you include the stranger, the fatherless, the widow, that you feed them at the table, and in so doing, you wrap them up as well in the love of our heavenly Father. This is a Christian discipline, one displayed and modeled all over God's word, and one we have to practice and practice and practice to get better at.

"All the days of the afflicted are evil, but he who is of a merry heart has a continual feast." —Proverbs 15:15

www.ingramcontent.com/pod-product-compliance
Lightning Source LLC
La Vergne TN
LVHW040852030125
800294LV00012B/323